PAIRING WINE WITH ASIAN FOOD

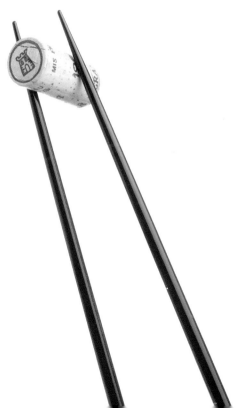

monsoonbooks

Published in 2009
by Monsoon Books Pte Ltd
52 Telok Blangah Road
#03-05 Telok Blangah House
Singapore 098829
www.monsoonbooks.com.sg

ISBN: 978-981-05-9213-4

Photography copyright © Collin Patrick / Black Studio (www.black.com.sg)

National Library Board Singapore Cataloguing in Publication Data
Soon, Edwin.
Pairing wine with Asian food / Edwin Soon. – Singapore : Monsoon, 2009.
p. cm.
Includes index.
ISBN-13 : 978-981-05-9213-4

1. Wine – Flavor and odor. 2. Wine and wine making. I. Title.
TX731
641.22 -- dc22   OCN221155977

Printed in Singapore

14 13 12 11 10 09   1 2 3 4 5 6 7 8 9

I could not have written this book without the inspiration and support of countless people. To the chefs, home cooks, wine lovers, wine merchants, wine boards, vignerons, wine producers, and various authors whose books and articles continue to enlighten me on my wine and food journey—thank you all! Thanks especially to Sandy Cheah, Daniel Chia, Joy Lee, Don Mendoza, Andrea Nguyen, Ming Pang, Collin Patrick, Jeff Sng, Soo Ah Kim, Jenny Tan, Tan Su Yen and Phil Tatham. Any errors in this book are mine and for that I apologize.

—Edwin Soon

Bottle of Château d'Yquem featured on page 52 kindly supplied by Vinum Fine Wine Merchant, Singapore (www.vinum.com.sg).

PAIRING WINE
WITH ASIAN FOOD

EDWIN SOON

monsoon

CONTENTS

INTRODUCTION

It used to be a simple affair matching wines with food: white wine with white meat; red wine with red meat. But that's for Western food. Venture into the Asian kitchen and things can begin to look complicated. But it needn't be.

Which wine would you choose to accompany a Thai green curry? Do you match the wine to the chicken or to the eggplant? What about the lemongrass and the coconut milk? And won't the fiery chili render your taste buds numb to the wine's subtle flavors?

Matching wines with Asian dishes can seem a daunting affair because there hasn't been a history of Asian cuisine evolving with wine. Yet the successful pairing of wine with Asian food is not an arcane undertaking. In this book, you will learn the most important theories and be well on your way to good food and wine liaisons.

First and foremost is to observe the taste relationship of the food with the wine—the saltiness, sweetness, sourness, and bitterness in food; and the sweetness, sourness, and bitterness in the wine.

Understanding this relationship and knowing whether to match or contrast the sweetness or the saltiness or sourness will enable you to make good judgment calls whenever you're selecting a wine to go with your Asian meal.

In a hurry? Just flip the pages of this book to the section entitled "An Occasion to Remember" where dishes are categorized by theme (for example, a finger food party) and type (such as curries or seafood).

Delve deeper into this book and you will find checklists of ideal wines to have in the cellar when you next cook Asian. In "A Serve of Asia", some of Asia's classic dishes are easily matched to suggested wines.

Whether you're a wine lover or new to the subject, this book encourages you to have fun and experiment. After all, wines are meant to be enjoyed with food, especially now with Asian food.

Edwin Soon
Singapore

UNDERSTANDING ASIAN FLAVORS

In pairing wine with Asian food, it helps to have an understanding of the taste components, textures, sensations, and flavors of Asian dishes as well as those of wine.

When the wine and dish are matched for all of the above, a heavenly marriage is achieved. The food and wine will sing in the mouth and bring smiles all around at the table.

Components

In food, especially Asian food, there are sweet, sour, salty, and bitter tastes. Call it the components if you like. Salty components in dishes come from salted fish, dried oysters, fish sauce, yellow and black bean paste, and soy. Think sweet and we mean honey, barbecue sauce, mirin, and plum sauce. Lemon juice, vinegar, and tamarind come to mind when we refer to the sour components in Asian dishes. Some foods are bitter such as petai bean (*parkia speciosa*), Thai eggplant, bittergourd, and several other herbs.

Why do we have to pay attention to the components? This is because wine reacts differently to the sweet, sour, salty, and bitter tastes in Asian food. Chew on a piece of green mango, and then take a sip of a generic white wine. You'll find that the wine tastes sweeter and seems unbalanced. At the same time, you'll probably cringe from the sourness of the mango. This sourness is accentuated by wine. The reason? Sour green mango makes the wine taste relatively sweeter and flabby. The effect is similar with salty foods. Sweet foods too will also change the taste of wine and usually makes wines that are not sweet, taste sour.

Textures

What's your taste in meat? Do you like it pulled, stringy and almost crispy, like that served with Thai rice, or in all its fatty glory as in a Chinese pork knuckle stew? Food has textures that can be light (steamed fish), rich (coconut-based curries), coarse (peanut sauce, fried tofu skins), and fatty (barbecued pork, wagyu beef). They can be matched accordingly to appropriate wines.

Stirfried food with crunchy textures can be enjoyed with fruity white wines or light red wines of fine consistency. Curries and stews with rich moist texture are best with red wines with rich texture or full-bodied white wines with high alcohol. This is discussed in the following chapter.

Sensations

Do you have a taste for the piquant where you need to add fresh chopped garlic, or a slice of ginger or even chili to your dish? These are the sensations of food in the mouth that have to be considered when matching wines with food. For example, the tartness of a dry wine often accentuates the chili sensations, as will the tannins in a red wine with high alcohol.

Flavors and Intensity

From the herbal scents of lemongrass and malty taste of miso to the exotic aromas of five spice and lychees, the flavors of food need also to be considered. Ensure that flavors do not clash, even though you have matches of the components and the textures and sensations.

Fortunately, flavor matching is usually easy. For example, a youthful Merlot exhibits plum-currant characteristics whilst a Syrah often has raspberry and blackberry aromas. Either wine, with their strong fruit characteristics, have flavors that easily meld with those of say, roasted duck with plum sauce, because the dark fruit flavors in both are complementary.

Similarly, sweet and sour dishes or food basted with honey easily finds complementary flavors in a young Chardonnay, which might have pineapple, lychee, peach, and butter overtones.

When matching by flavor, it is important to match intensities of flavor in both food and wine or one will overcome the other in flavor.

Heavenly Marriage

Imagine serving an aged Riesling with some tangy crisp acidity and citrus mineral-oil flavors alongside a steamed river fish with ginger, soy, and chili. The citrus-tart nature of the wine contrasts the salty soy in the dishes. The wine's fine consistency is matched to the fish's delicate texture. The wine's citrus flavor is a counterpoint to the ginger and soy tastes whilst the light sweetness in the wine parries the chili. This is a match in components, textures, sensations, and flavor!

PROBLEM INGREDIENTS

Chili

Alcohol in wine and chili in food can clash. Wine contains alcohol which has a warming effect in the mouth. Wines with high alcohol content can exacerbate the heat in the mouth. Chili contains capsaicin—the source of the burning sensation. Alcohol can spread the chili sensations around the mouth making everything taste hotter than ever.

The solution? Low alcohol wines. German wines are famous for having low alcohol content. Another option is to use sweet wines to tame the fire—the sugar soothes the burn. Alternatively, bubbly wines can be called upon for some cleansing action—the tangy acidity cleans the palate and stimulates the taste buds whilst the bubbles accentuate and refresh.

Souring Agents

Sour foods such as tamarind, green mango, and lime make wines taste flat and flabby. Beware when serving wines with Asian dishes featuring pomelo and other sour ingredients.

Umami

Umami is the fifth taste. Discovered by Professor Ikeda in the early 1900s, umami explains why certain foods taste delicious and its origin has been traced to natural amino acid, glutamic acid, or glutamates found in meats, fish, cheese, tomatoes and other protein-heavy foods.

Keep chewy/tannic red wines away from seafood. The tannins of red wine will react with the umami-savory tastes in the seafood to bring out metallic tastes leaving a dry, rough sensation in your mouth. Dried shrimp is a common ingredient in Chinese, Korean, Indochinese, and Southeast Asian cuisine, whose umami taste is released when reconstituted and/or cooked with other ingredients.

When seafood dishes have light sauces the umami effect will be strongest. Serve white wines or, if you must have some color, pink wines with very low tannins will work just as well.

Vinegar has the same effect as sour fruits and can kill the taste in wine. However, most Asian dishes that employ vinegar have balancing ingredients such as soy, sugar and other ingredients. If you detect strong sour components in the food, the best wines to choose are those that are light, crisp, and tart. As long as the wine tastes sharper than the souring agent in the food, it will never fall flat. Wines to try are Aligote, Bacchus, Chasselas, Chenin Blanc, Müller Thurgau, Muscadet, Picpoul de Pinet, Patrimonio, Quincy, Soave Classico, Sylvaner, and wines with the term "trocken" or "brut".

Dark Spices

Tannic red wines are usually bitter. When paired with dishes that have bitter elements or dark spices, wines' tannins and bitterness feed off the dish's bitter or spicy elements, accentuating bitter tastes. Tannic wines therefore do not work with foods that are heavily spiced with cardamom, cinnamon, star anise, cumin, turmeric, as well as many of the herbs found in Thai cuisine.

Numbing Ingredients

"Ma la" in Chinese describes the numbing and spicy flavor common in Sichuan cooking, derived from using a combination of Sichuan pepper and chili. It is the Sichuan pepper (similar to Japanese sansho pepper) or the pod of the Zanthoxylum fruits (*Z. piperitum*, *Z. simulans* and *Z. schinifolium*) that causes the unique tingly numbness in the mouth. Few wines can stand up to this so wait for the sensation to subside before partaking in wine. If you must, a strongly sweet syrupy wine can be served— no guarantees here though!

Fermented ingredients

Beware of fermented ingredients like kimchi and fermented soybean. Fermented shrimp paste or "belacan/trassi" features in most cuisines in Southeast Asia under various guises. The strong aftertaste of fermented ingredients (often with added chili) affects your palate's ability to fully enjoy your wine. It's here that iced water works best but fortified sweet wines like Sherry or Port (served on the rocks) can be divine!

WINE'S VARIED TASTES

When serving wine with a meal, it is helpful to understand the varied tastes in wine—how a wine's sweetness, dryness, tannins, alcohol, weight, and flavor signature interact with the tastes of food.

Wine's Components

Pick up any wine and take a sip. In the first two seconds of the wine in your mouth, you will determine whether the wine tastes sweet or dry (not sweet). There are thousands of wines in the world and most of them can be categorized as sweet or dry.

Dry Wines

Dry white wines can have low acidity. The low acid wines of Viognier and Pinot Grigio often play a secondary role in food and wine liaisons—they let the dish take the lead in taste.

Other high acidity wines are tangy and take on a contrasting role. They can highlight the savory taste of food. Salt in food "pushes" taste (something chefs are well aware of) whilst acid "pulls" taste—hence a balance is achieved when a tangy wine is served with a salty dish.

With oily Asian dishes, a higher acidity wine helps to penetrate the fat to reveal the flavors beneath. Tangy-tart wines that cut through the oil in rich dishes can also cleanse the palate, wiping off piquant chili tastes, so we can enjoy the experience of the plush and/or fiery dish without surfeit of it. Choose from Albariño to Viura and wines with the words "brut" or "trocken" displayed on the label. See chart on page 15 for a complete listing.

Lightly Sweet Wines

Sweet wines sit happily alongside most dishes, often blending into the taste of the dish. At the very least they perform just like a soda smoothly washing down the kung pao chicken or yakitori. Sweet wines come in lightly sweet and strongly sweet versions.

Wines that are lightly sweet marry well with many Asian dishes because they contrast the savory aspects of food. They include Moscato, sparkling wines labeled demi-sec, red Lambrusco and the pink-colored White Zinfandel. See chart on page 15 for a complete listing.

Strongly Sweet Wines

Strongly sweet wines are not quite as versatile. Although they work with many dishes, their sugary nature and strong flavors can overshadow any delicate tastes in food. Choose from ice wine to sweet Sherries. See chart on page 15 for a complete listing.

Texture and Tannin

Higher acidity wines can highlight the textures of food. Taste-wise, a tangy and bubbly wine has the same effect as a squeeze of lemon on crispy batter fried food- with an additional role; its effervescence mirrors the crispy texture of the food.

Wine tannins come from fermentation involving grape skins and maturation of wine in oak barrels. Tannins have a bitter taste but, as a sensation of touch, are experienced as astringency. In essence it is a puckering feeling in the mouth, similar to that when we eat unsweetened chocolate or chew on the skins and seeds of fruits. Red wines come in low tannin and high tannin versions.

Low Tannin Red Wines

Low tannin red wines such as Beaujolais, Tempranillo, and Valpolicella and can make good partners for Asian dishes. Their interaction with food is similar to dry white wines. Low tannin red wines, especially those with a tangy acidity (e.g. Gamay, Grignolino, Barbera), can be served with seafood. See chart on page 15 for a complete listing.

High Tannin Red Wines

The high tannin red wines such as Bordeaux, Barolo, and Zinfandel have difficulties when matching with seafood. When tannin and fish oils interact, an undesirable metallic taste arises.

However, tannic red wines are a perfect partner for meat and creamy dishes. Tannins naturally seek out proteins and fats to bind with. Tannic wines are thus a natural cohort with dishes that are high in proteins and fats such as red meat or creamy gravies. The result is a smoother tasting wine and delicate tasting food.

Note that many vegetarian dishes lack proteins or fats. A red wine's tannins will react with the proteins on the tongue and sides of the mouth—accentuating the bitterness and bringing about an astringent taste.

Body, Warmth and Weight

Wine has the component of alcohol. Alcohol gives wine some added texture but alcohol also can be sensed as a warm feeling in the mouth. After swallowing a wine, you will notice if the wine is alcoholic or not—some wines leave a warm sensation (high alcohol) whilst others are unnoticeable.

The body or weight of a wine should be thought of as its relative "thickness" or viscosity. A wine can be light and thin, medium, or heavy and full. The body of a wine is made up of its alcohol content, its tannin and sugar content. Typically wines with higher alcohol levels are perceived to have more density and

texture and can be described as weightier.

Most dry white wines are light bodied. Exceptions are Chardonnay, Viognier, Roussanne, Grenache Blanc, and oaked Sauvignon Blancs. Judging from their consistency or viscosity, they are dry and medium-heavy bodied white wines. Strongly sweet wines are syrupy and are heavyweight.

In terms of food pairing, you can match the consistency/body/weight of the wine to the body of the food. Big alcohol and tannic red wines (full body) such as Shiraz or Zinfandel, pair well with a hearty dish such as raan (Indian roasted spicy lamb) or a braised goose. The wine tastes dense from the alcohol and matches the dish's weight. Additionally, the wine's tannins react positively with the meat.

Flavors

Each wine style has a flavor signature. The flavors range from the fruity and smoky to the herbal, spicy, and earthy. Each works differently with food although this is not the most important aspect of food and wine matching.

Mind these tips

☞ Low alcohol or lightly sweet sparkling wines almost always can be served with a variety of Asian dishes. Choose from the low alcohol Clairette de Die from France's Rhone region and Sovetskoe Shampansko, the semi-sweet sparkling wine from Russia and the former Soviet states, to the ubiquitous spumantes from Italy.

☞ In the absence of a white wine or light reds, serving red wines chilled at between 11 to 15 degrees centigrade will reduce the sensation of tannin, therefore increasing a degree of union with, say, a delicate fish.

☞ Watch out for sweet foods—fruit-based, sweet sour sauce, barbecue sauce, plum sauce, honey, etc—as they can strip a wine of its fruity flavors and make it seem sour, tannic, or bitter. Sometimes the oil in dishes can play havoc with the sweet wine—dry and tart white wines are a better choice.

☞ It is not necessary to always mirror sour tastes in food with tart wines. In fact, a highly acidic wine with a dish cooked with acidic vegetables or vinegar will make both the wine and dish seem unpalatable due to the combined acidity despite the expectation of reciprocity.

MAKING THE MATCH

When serving wine with a meal, it's helpful to think of the role you want the wine to play. Is it merely to slake your thirst or cleanse the palate or is the wine the highlight and the food an accompaniment? The following are ten concepts—from the easiest to the more complex—to bear in mind when attempting a match.

1. Slake that thirst
It is easiest to wash down a salty dish with dry white wine or a sweet one. Sparkling wines are a good bet too. They can be brut (dry), demi-sec (off-dry or lightly sweet), and doux (sweet). When in doubt, go for a sweet wine as it offers more possibilities of a good match.

2. Echo the flavors; flatter tastes
Serve nutty and oaked wines with food featuring sesame oil, coconut and peanut curries. Flatter the salty or spicy dishes with fruity wines.

3. Maintain equality
Don't allow the food to overpower the wine or vice versa. Seek balance in the intensity of flavors.

4. Let one take the lead
If the food is intricate, do not overcome its subtle tastes with a wine that is intensely flavored and big bodied; a simple and light wine alongside lets the food tastes shine. Conversely, accompany an expensive, fine, well-matured complex wine with a simple dish so that the wine takes the limelight.

5. Match cooking methods
Fine, light delicate wines work with poached or steamed food that has light textures and tastes. Match flavorsome and medium bodied wines with grilled food, roasts and stews

6. Use contrast
Salty and umami dishes show well with dry white wines. Highlight salty flavors with tangy-tart wines.

7. Consider textures
Mirror crisp fried foods with crisp white wines. Contrast rich fatty foods with a dry white wine. Match textures of rich dishes with a big bodied, wine. Tannic wines like oily and rich dishes as the tannins bind with the fat and protein.

8. Sweetness is a good thing
Sweet wines can match most savory dishes by complementing the spices and muting any chili piquancy. Like sugar for coffee, a sweet wine will also balance and match any bitterness in food. A dish of roasted eggplants drizzled with hot sesame oil garlic and chili will find a match in a sweet wine.

9. Tartness is just as good
Acid in wine is responsible for a "lively" sharp sensation. A tangy wine works just like a lime juice might, in contrasting a rich stew, enabling you to taste the intensity of the dish. Dry tangy wines will also find a liaison with the tart tastes in food (lemon, tamarind); contrast with the sweet items in food (Indonesian kecap manis, Japanese mirin, sugar); tone down the texture of oil (tuna belly, fried crispy lard); feed off the heat (ginger, garlic) and highlight savory aspects in food (fish sauce, soy sauce, miso, prawn paste). Tart wines also mitigate the oiliness and rich textures of food items such as fried samosas and spring rolls.

10. Complement and compliment food and wine
Mature wines (flavors of mushrooms, meat, soy in red wines; honey and preserved fruit in white wines) will complement strong flavored meats. Barbecued seafood or roasted meat has smoky aromas and can be matched to aged Bordeaux or Cabernet Sauvignon with earthy, leather and soy overtones. Similarly, barbecued food will also pair nicely with a spicy Rhone wine or a barrel-aged smoky Chardonnay. Barbecued seafood provides enough oily textures and flavors to stand up to a hefty red wine such as a New World Shiraz.

Wine Style	Dry Wines (still & sparkling)	Lightly Sweet Wines (still & sparkling)	Strongly Sweet Wines	Low Tannin Red Wines	High Tannin Red Wines
Wine	Albariño • Bacchus • Chablis • Chenin Blanc • Chardonnay (unoaked) • Chardonnay (oak) • Colombard • Entre-deux-Mers • Frascati • Furmint • Gavi • Grenache Blanc • Grüner Veltliner • Müller Thurgau • Muscadet • Orvieto • Picpoul de Pinet • Pinot Blanc • Pinot Grigio • Rioja • Roussanne • Sauvignon Blanc • Fumé/Sauvignon Blanc (oak) • Soave • Tocai Friulano • Trebbiano • Verdelho • Vinho Verde • Viognier • Viura • dry Semillon • dry Riesling Wines with any of these terms on the label: secco, trocken or brut. Fino Sherry • Oloroso Sherry Dry pink/rosé wines, and wines with the term vin gris, blush, saignée or weißherbst.	Asti • Cadillac • Cerons • Gewürztraminer • Loupiac • Moscato • Moscatel • St Croix du Monts Wines with any of these terms on the label: abboccato, amabile, demi-sec, doux, halbtrocken, lieblich, spätlese. Brachetto d'Acqui, Marzemino and Lambrusco are red wines that are sweet, whilst White Zinfandel is a pink still wine. Medium Sherry	Barsac • Eiswein • Coteaux du Layon • Monbazillac • Muscat • Sauternes • Torcolato • Tokaji Wines with any of these terms on the label: ausbruch, auslese, beerenauslese, botrytis, doux, dulce, late harvest, moelleux, noble rot, passito, recioto, selections grains nobles, trockenbeerenauslese, vendange tardive and vin de glaciere. Banyuls • Port • sweet/Cream Sherry • Vin Doux Naturel • Vin Santo	Barbaresco • Barbera • Bardolino • Beaujolais • Bourgueil • Cabernet Franc • Carignan • Chianti • Chinon • Cotes du Rhone • Gamay • Grignolino • Grenache • Minervois • Merlot Montepulciano d'Abruzzo • Nero d'Avola • Pinot Noir & Red Burgundy • Ribera del Duero • Rioja • Sangiovese • Tempranillo • Valpolicella	Aglianico • Barolo • Bordeaux and Côtes de Bordeaux • Côtes de Blaye • Côtes de Castillon • Cabernet Sauvignon • Cahors • Cornas • Côtes Rôtie • Dolcetto (oak) • Hermitage • Malbec • Mourvèdre • Petit Verdot • Petite Sirah • Primitivo • Sagrantino • St Emilion • Syrah/Shiraz • Tannat • Zinfandel Sparkling Shiraz
Cooking Methods	Steamed • poached • stirfried • deepfried	Stirfried • deepfried • grilled	Braised • grilled • roasted • steamed (with strong sauce)	Stirfried • braised • grilled • roasted	Stir fried • braised • grilled • roasted
Components, Textures, Sensations, & Flavors	Salty sauces • thick creamy gravies and curries • oily textures • fishy flavors • souring agents • vegetables	Salty sauces • nutty sauces • thick creamy gravies • sour ingredients • chili	Sweet and sour sauces • fiery chili • strong sauces • nuts • fermented ingredients • /numbing ingredients	Salty sauces • creamy gravies • fishy flavors • dark spices • chili	Creamy gravies • predominant red meat textures and flavors
Dishes	Sautéed fish slices • pakora • tomato pappu • curry kapitan • sashimi • saengseon hoe • hor mok	Spicy chicken wings • nasi goreng • sambal petai • sayur lodeh • mango kerabu • itek tim • laap • dum pukht	Pork and fermented beancurd • sukiyaki • nasi lemak • pork vindaloo • moong dal	Hunan crispy duck • korma • babi guling • kaldereta • kodi pulao	Mongolian lamb • rendang • teppanyaki • beef stew picadillo • kebabs

FAVORITE WINES FOR ASIAN FLAVORS

Weighty white wines for dishes with sweet overtones

Savory Asian dishes can have a predominant sweet taste. Choose dry wines with some weight and relatively higher alcohol such as Chardonnay, Fumé Blanc and Viognier for dishes from Shanghai, Indonesian Sudanese, South Vietnamese and Thai and Malaysian "lemak" or coconut-based curries. Hermitage Blanc (Marsanne-Roussanne blend) is another wine with weight and a gorgeous texture. With gindara teriyaki or grilled/baked silver cod with teriyaki sauce the wine simply glides over the tongue to make its union with the dish.

Lightly sweet Vouvray demi-sec for sour dishes

Savory and sour dishes feature prominently in Asian cuisine. Examples include Thai salads and Malaysian tamarind-based curries. Mulligatawny is an Anglo–Indian soup meaning pepper water. It is reminiscent of the South Indian rasam, and was created by the servants for the British Raj. Although it has a savory taste of garlic, onions, curry powder, and vegetables, it's predominantly tangy due to a healthy dose of tamarind or lemon juice, tempered by a dash of yogurt or cream. Vouvray demi sec—a lightly sweet wine with bubbles makes the match in many ways. The cold wine with bubbles makes a temperature and textural contrast to the hot soup. The wine's sweetness and fruit contrast the soup's sourness and spice. Opposites attract here.

Champagne and sparkling wines for salty dishes

Dry wines are right in sync with salty Asian flavors. Their penetrating acidity and clean fruit flavors sit well with soy and fish sauce. If the wine has bubbles, there is the additional cleansing action for any chili piquancy. Bubbles also add textural interest and contrast for crispy fried foods. It's no wonder dry sparkling wines and Champagnes are the ideal wines for dishes ranging from crispy bee hoon and crab soup, spicy Thai steamed mussels and sambal ikan masin (spicy sour salted fish).

Tempranillo with low tannin for strong flavored and spicy dishes

What do Nonya dishes like Too Huwait Char Kuchai (chives with black pudding), Gulai Pak Lai (giblet curry), Perut Ikan (picked fish stomach curry) and the Thai dish of Sai Krok Isan (Thai issan sour fermented pork balls) have in common? All these dishes have unusually pungent tastes. Spanish red wines made from Tempranillo, with fine tannins, and flavors reminiscent of cranberries and cherries, and a touch of vanilla-toast - are the answer.

Moscato, lightly sweet for piquant chili

The more heat a dish packs, the lower the alcohol level should be in the wine. This is so that a balance can be achieved between the fiery chili element of the dish and the alcohol level of the accompanying wine. Pla Ra Bong is a north-eastern Thai dish made from fermented fish and ground roasted rice. Essentially a nam prik or chili paste dip of the Northeast. The extreme fire demands not only a low alcohol sweet wine but one that is sweet. So, Moscato is the wine of choice here.

Grüner Veltliner for vegetables

Few wines are friendly to vegetables. Austria's Grüner Veltliner is one such wine that fits the bill here. Its zippy acidity, lowish alcohol, clarity of flavors—white pepper, vegetables, citrus, pear, quince and apple, spicy green peppers—deem it a wine for vegetarian dishes, especially umami-rich dried salty vegetables and other preserved Asian vegetables. Moreover, Grüner Veltliner is known to be good with "difficult" vegetables such as artichokes and asparagus. Some excellent matches of this wine are to be had with zaru soba (chilled soba), stir fried vegetables in oyster sauce, and sesame-flavored salads.

Rosé wine and multi-textured dishes

Rosé wine is one of those flexible wines that take up with various food types and flavors. It's at home with white meats and seafood and doesn't complain when asked to accompany red meats. It handles spices incredibly well, as well as herbs and aromatics. Consider banh mi, the Vietnamese sandwich. It has complex flavors and textures—there's vinegar, radish, sugar, onions, pork, liver pate, cucumber, chili, mayonnaise, and more. Wash it all down with a slurp of pink wine!

Off-dry Riesling for complex flavors

Poh piah is the Singapore version of the Fujian spring roll, that features diverse ingredients including yambean, shallots, beansprouts beancurd, garlic, prawns, and lettuce—topped with peanuts, chili, and sweet dark sauce. Rieslings come in various versions – trocken (dry), spätlese (lightly sweet), 'vendange tardive' (sweet), and 'selections grains nobles' / auslese / beerenauslese / ice wine (syrupy sweet). Choose your wine according to how much sweet sauce you add to the Poh Piah. The sweeter the dish, the sweeter the wine should be.

Red Burgundy for meaty and sweet spicy flavors

The mahogany-gold colored,

Hong Kong roast squab is salty, sweet, gamey, five spice-scented, spicy with a hint of ginger and with vinegar-soy glazed crisp skin. It calls for a wine with seductive stone fruit aromas and earthy overtones but with ripe acids and fine tannins and a lingering finish—hence a Burgundy.

Oloroso Sherry for nutty flavors

With flavors of roasted nuts, vanilla, and warm caramel, with a slight sweetness, but with a creamy texture and hint of tangy fruit on the finish, Oloroso Sherry is the perfect mate for satay beef stir-fry. The wine mirrors the peanut and coconut-milk gravy of the stir-fry, without being over come by the garlic, ginger, shrimp paste, and curry spices used.

Pinot Grigio or Pinot Gris for delicate seafood and stronger sauces

This wine has two faces depending on its alcohol content. One version is zippy, vibrant, with pleasant lemon freshness and crisp mineral acidity—the perfect foil for fried seafoods, tempura, sushi, sashimi and Chinese steamed

Mind these tips

A common mistake when matching wine with food is that of resemblance. That a Gewürztraminer, because of its spicy characteristics, should accompany curry is a misunderstanding of flavor matching. The pungency of both may be equal in intensity but the opposing spice elements aggravate the incompatibility. Red wines such as Merlot, Nero d'Avola, or Zinfandel, with strong berry flavors, are unexpected matches as the bold fruit in the wines play up to the curry spices.

German wine labels indicate the ripeness level when the grapes were picked and/or the residual sugar of the wine. 'Spätlese' refers to wine made from grapes picked ripe / harvested late. Wines are correspondingly sweet. 'Spätlese' wines can be designated 'trocken' that means that wine has been fermented until little residual sugar remains, implying a dry wine.

fish. Choose from unoaked or mildly oak-influenced Pinot Gris or Pinot Grigio from Italy, California, Oregon, New Zealand (lower alcohol ones) and the German Rulander or Grauburgunder.

The other style is Pinot Gris from Alsace (until recently called Tokay Pinot Gris) and includes some fuller-bodied higher alcohol versions from New Zealand and Australia.

These wines are totally adept in handling the strong flavors of - sweet and sour; meat with hoisin sauce; Thai lemongrass dishes; Indian spiced dishes featuring coriander, cumin and ginger; and the sweet-soy-vinegar or the sesame-oil and rice wine seasonings in Shanghai dishes.

AN OCCASION TO REMEMBER

DISHES LISTED BY THEME

Dim Sum

Think steamed siew mai, fried tofu skins, and braised pork ribs for great-tasting Chinese finger-food. The light seafood and pork flavors are best accompanied by a Chardonnay that is not too oaky; try a French Vin de Pays or a Sicilian Chardonnay–Insolia blend. For a special treat, pair dim sum with a glass of Blanc de Blancs Champagne.

PARTY FOODS

Spice up your next drinks party by serving Asian snacks and wine. With such a variety of small bites to choose from, the permutations are endless. Chinese dim sum, Indian samosa, and Thai fish cakes are obvious choices, and for good reason, but don't forget to look at Vietnamese spring rolls, Japanese octopus dumplings, Korean gimbap, and Malaysian fried bananas. Just go easy on the dips, which can cause havoc with your choice of wine.

Crispy Roast Pig

Go easy on the plum sauce, so as not to overpower the wine, and you can get away with many types of white wine such as a light smoky Pinot Gris, a crisp Riesling with a bit of age, or a Chardonnay. You could even try a rosé.

Lumpia

Crispy vegetarian (or pork) spring rolls from the Philippines, dipped in salty soy sauce, love the counterpoint of a crisp, tangy white wine. Australian Semillon fits the bill.

Vietnamese Spring Roll

Bursting with flavor and packed with vegetables and shrimp, the ideal wine should be crisp and tangy. Serve a Sauvignon Blanc.

Samosa

The perfect party food, Indian samosas can be filled with a variety of ingredients and can be mild to extra hot. If the curry flavors are subtle, serve a dry wine, or a palate-cleansing, crisp and dry or sweet but low-alcohol sparkling wine such as Cava or Spumante.

Vada Pau

Surprise guests by serving a chilled Port to counter the complex flavors of this South Asian potato ball, coated with green chilies, ginger, mustard seeds, turmeric, and chutney.

Pakora

Although there are many varieties of pakora in South Asia, two popular ones are palak pakora (spinach) and paneer pakora (cottage cheese). A medium dry wine such as a rosé from France's Anjou region is a fun choice.

Korokke

Go easy on the sour, sweet, and savory tonkatsu sauce, which is served with these Japanese deep-fried croquettes. Pick a sweet wine with acidity such as a German spätlese, or better still, an auslese.

Onogiri

Japanese rice balls with nori are slightly salty and sour due to the umeboshi (pickled Japanese apricot). Beaujolais will pick up on the salt and the fruit.

Gimbap

Similar in appearance to sushi rolls, Korean gimbap is nutty from the sesame oil, sweet and sour from the vinegar and sugar seasonings added to the rice. A complex dish that requires a simple wine. Serve any red or white you have on hand.

Pisang Goreng

For a sinfully sweet snack try these delicious Malaysian batter-coated bananas with a sweet wine such as Canadian ice wine.

Gado-gado

The peanut sauce and spice in this popular Indonesian salad demands a light or a syrupy sweet wine. A late-harvest Riesling works best with the sweeter salad from East Java but is equally at home with the salty West Javanese one.

Bindaetteok

This Korean mung bean pancake with scallions and kimchi or chili calls for a lightly sweet pink wine such as White Zinfandel.

Takoyaki

Japanese baked or fried battered octopus balls, topped with okonomiyaki sauce, aonori seaweed, mayonnaise, and fish shavings is mushy, creamy, crunchy, savory, and sour. A dry nutty Fino Sherry makes a textural connection as well as a counterpoint in taste.

Kir, the French cocktail made with a measure of crème de cassis topped up with any dry white wine, works with most party foods.

Red Duck Curry

A Merlot makes a good match to this medium-hot red curry from Thailand as the flavors of stone fruit in the wine make a strong liaison with the meaty flavors of the duck.

CURRIES

Use wine as a simple but refreshing counterpoint to a fragrant curry. The best wines to serve are fruity whites, and chilled low-tannin, fruity reds. When the curry is redolent with piquant chili, the wine should be sweet to balance the hot chili. However, lower alcohol red wines from Switzerland, or German white wines, need not be as sweet and can still hold the heat well. Alternatively, try the cleansing action of a tart white wine such as Australian Semillon, Chablis or a Muscadet.

Green Chicken Curry

This Thai dish can be fiery, and has flavors of coconut and basil. A woody Chardonnay works best with green curry; the wine has the same textural thickness as the curry weight while its buttery notes respond to the coconut milk in the curry without competing with it.

Masala Fish Curry

Dry masala fish curry calls for delicate wines with lemony acidity. Try Italian Verdicchio, Spanish Albariño or a slim and steely Müller-Thurgau

Kashmiri Chicken Korma

A red wine with medium tannins will meld with the cream whilst the wine's fruit signature will highlight the mild spices. Spanish Tempranillo, a Saumur or a Beaujolais Cru will flatter the dish.

Chicken Tikka Masala

Dubbed the national dish of Britain, chicken tikka masala (and fish prepared in the same style) is slightly smoky from the tandoor cooking whilst the masala sauce is well spiced, rich, and creamy, but not fiery hot. A sparkling Shiraz served here is a contrast in texture and taste.

Vindaloo

This classic Indian curry features vinegar, which brings to the spices, and chili heat, an unforgettable sour taste. Balance it all with a lightly sweet red sparkling wine called Marzemino, which comes from Trentino in Italy. Otherwise, anything pink will do.

Goan Seafood Curry

When dining on this ever popular Goan dish, pink and rosé wines such as Cerasuolo Montepulciano d'Abruzzo bring an unpretentious elegance to the table.

Curry Kapitan

Mild, creamy and succulent, this Eurasian chicken dish from Malaysia is easily accompanied by rich textured white wines such as Viognier, Marsanne, and Chardonnay.

Curry Debal

Portuguese devil curry from Malacca is a rich and fiery hot dish, made with mustard powder, turmeric powder, vinegar, candlenuts, and lots of chilies. Chicken, pork and occasionally wild boar, could feature but ultimately, it's the hot curry you have to match. Go with a sweet Muscat or a sweet Greek Mavrodaphne.

Rendang

Dry rendang curries are dark brown and are the signature Indonesian/Malaysian curry. For this thick coconut curry, you can uncork tannic and big wines. Cabernet Sauvignon, Bordeaux, and Barolo have their place here.

Gulai Kambing

A toasty oak-aged Chardonnay can be served with Indonesian lamb curry, with its flavors of lemongrass, coconut milk, lime leaves, ginger, and dark spices. Otherwise, a Châteauneuf du Pape red wine, with nuances of leather and earth over small red fruits is a good bet.

Opor Ayam

This yellow-colored (turmeric) Indonesian coconut milk chicken curry is nutty and creamy with a fresh galangal-cilantro-lemongrass taste. It will take to light red wines such as St Laurent or Pinot Noir. Otherwise, venture a pink wine.

Brachetto d'Acqui, from Piedmonte, Italy, works with most curries. It is lightly sweet, mildly bubbly, with low alcohol, and tastes of raspberries, strawberries, cranberries, roses, and grapes.

Chili Crab

The robust, rich, dense, and full-flavored sauce of this Singapore classic calls for an equally weighty wine. A chilled Liqueur Muscat, sweet and rich, will make the match. However a fruity red such as Lambrusco with some residual sweetness will also work.

SEAFOOD

The iodine in raw crustaceans has an affinity for young wines that are tangy and extremely dry such as Sauvignon Blanc, Muscadet, Riesling, and Sylvaner. When crustaceans are cooked, the iodine is masked and aromas become more complex so a mature or richer wine can be used. Cold, cooked lobster and quality, aged Chardonnay is a perfect match. Fish and wine present few problems, it is more a case of matching the wine to the sauce or condiments.

Lobster Beehoon

The rich seafood stock in this unusual but sublime Singaporean dish with savory garlic tastes finds its partner in a textured wine with white fruit nuances such as a Viognier.

Teochew Cold Crab

Beware of the vinegar dip that does little to show subtle wines in the best light. Serve a sweetish wine such as a Gewürztraminer or Moscato.

Steamed Bamboo Clams

Bamboo (or razor) clams steamed with minced garlic or a sweetish garlic sauce is a delicate dish. Pair this dish with Semillon or white Cassis.

Grilled Sea Scallops with Fermented Black Beans

This dish brims with flavor. There are light bitter nuances from the beans, nutty notes from the sesame oil and cooking method, heat from the garlic, ginger, and rice wine. Add to that a lift from the cilantro garnish and lime wedge. A match of this complexity is achieved from the contrasts of components, textures, sensations and temperatures with a Reserve Chardonnay or a Grand Cru white Burgundy—no less.

Ikan Nila Goreng

This Indonesian deepfried fish with sambal of tamarind and chili needs a spätlese Riesling with enough acidity to contrast the crispy fish, and a little sweetness to envelope the hot chili sambal.

Fish Pilaf

Imagine a fish rice dish, scented with cumin, cloves, cardamoms, cinnamon, red chili, coriander, and tamarind—bright and dark flavors, lively and savory, and a little warm. Serve a dry Hungarian Furmint with apple and grapefruit aromas, good acidity but a velvety texture from the alcohol. Otherwise, try Pinot Blanc or a Tarrango (red).

Penang Cuttlefish Salad

Broiled cuttlefish with kangkong (water convolvulus) topped with a sweet, spicy sauce and sprinkled with crispy shallots and crushed peanuts is on the sweet side. So head for sweet wines such as Muscat or the Vino di Santo of Santorini, Greece.

Haemul-Pajeon

A delicious Korean seafood pancake or omelet with lots of chopped scallions. Serve a Pinot Grigio. Red wines are a tough call no matter how fruity they are because of the shrimp/squid.

Cucumber & Bagoong Salad

This Filipino dish has forward and strong tastes and a wine needs to stand up to the salted and fermented fish in the bagoong. Gewürztraminer or a Sauvignon Blanc work here.

Thod Mun Pla

Thai fish cakes require something aromatic such as a Sauvignon Blanc, or better, a Vermentino from Italy or Corsica.

Yum Talay

The Laotian version of this seafood salad features squid, mussels, and shrimp with fish sauce, lime, onions, and cilantro,. Try a Rosato from Tuscany, made from Sangiovese grapes, with lots of red berry flavors, some tartness and a smooth finish.

With seafood dishes where sauces and dips are used sparingly, most of these wines make good pairings: Arneis, Bourgogne Aligoté, Cremant de Bourgogne, Cortese di Gavi, Muscadet, Tocai Fruilano, Frascati, Orvieto, Fino Sherry, Sancerre, Silvaner, Soave, and Torrontes. Try also these affordable Chardonnay-based White Burgundies: Petit Chablis, Mâcon-Villages, St. Veran, Viré-Clessé, Bouzeron, Rully, Mercurey, Givry, and Montagny.

Satay

Satay, or sate, consists of chunks of turmeric-manirated meat (chicken, goat, mutton, beef, pork, fish, rabbit, etc) threaded onto bamboo or coconut-leaf-spine skewers, grilled over a wood or charcoal fire, then served with a spicy peanut dip. For Malaysian satay, try a light white wine that will play a background role. For Indonesian satay, with its soy-based dip, opt for a fruity blended generic red. For pork satay with its spicy sweet pineapple-based peanut sauce, try the characterful match of Ice-wine, Barsac, Vouvray Moelleux or even a chilled Ruby or Tawny Port.

ASIAN BARBECUE

Asia has a strong tradition of grilling food, from simple skewers of satay cooked over a portable burner on a street corner to lavish Korean barbecue spreads comprising a medley of meat and seafood, and a large number side dishes, pickles, and sauces. The flavors of Asian grills are easy to replicate on the backyard barbecue or kitchen hibachi and wine is a natural accompaniment to the smoke and spice. California Zinfandel and Chinese char siew is a must-try combination.

Thai Kai Yang

Originating from northeast Thailand, this chicken is marinated in a melody of aromatic Thai spices and then barbecued. Applied sparingly, the accompanying chili sauce will not interfere with an oaked white. Choose from amongst Chardonnays, Fumé Blancs, or Pinot Blancs.

Char Siew

Take a bite of succulent Chinese barbecued pork ribs glistening with sweet and spicy red marinade (hoisin, black bean paste, sugar, five spice), then, sip on a California Zinfandel with its jammy aromas of raspberry, liquorice, and pepper tang. The Zinfandel has ample tannin to handle the meat's fat well, and its fullness and fruitiness blend into the dish's taste. A delicious combination!

Seekh Kebab

Punjabi comfort food cooked over hot coals, the sausage-like textured lamb is flavored with garam masala, smoke, and more. Uncork a smooth Merlot or a Shiraz/Syrah from New Zealand, Australia, California or South Africa.

Kalbi

Kalbi may refer to the grilled ribs but it is really a Korean banquet over a charcoal grill, surrounded by various salads, rice, and pickles. The barbecued meat is cut into small pieces and wrapped in fresh lettuce leaves with rice, a thin slice of garlic, ssamjang (mixture of gochujang and dwenjang), and other seasonings. New World red wines with smooth tannins and residual sweetness such as Merlot blends or Cabernet blends or Shiraz blends work here, or venture a sweet Malmsey Madeira for something different.

Ikayaki

Japanese grilled squid is juicy and smoky, and is usually dipped in soy sauce.

Sauvignon Blanc—grassy, cool, and tangy—makes a great contrast in flavors.

Yakiniku

An assortment of bite-sized grilled meats—beef, offal, chicken, and pork—is barbecued and served with salt and lemon juice; a tare sauce, or with garlic- or miso-based dips. A tannic Touriga Nacional from Portugal works. Otherwise, California Orange Muscat or South Africa's Vin de Constance, served ice cold is a refreshing accompaniment.

Lechón

Very popular in the Philippines, lechón is a whole roasted pig, and here, wine choices are many. A Gewürztraminer, floral and spicy with a touch of sweet, accompanies the pig like a sauce. A Mouvèdre from France or Malbec from Argentina will be concentrated and work with the texture of the pig while other options include Australian sparkling Shiraz or California White Zinfandel. These wines also work with crispy pork pata (deepfried legs or pork).

Sambal Stingray

A popular dish in Singapore, stingray is marinated in ginger, tamarind, and shrimp paste then wrapped in a banana leaf and barbecued. Sambal chili and a squeeze of lime further enhances the barbecue flavors. A refreshing White Zinfandel with watermelon flavors and a sweet but tangy finish acts as a counterfoil to this complex tasting dish.

Fumé Blanc was popularized by Robert Mondavi and is a Sauvignon Blanc aged in wood, similar to the Pouilly-Fumé of the Loire Valley, France. Pouilly Fumé should not be confused with Pouilly Fuissé, a wine made from Chardonnay, in Burgundy.

A SERVE OF ASIA

DISHES LISTED BY COUNTRY

Beijing Roast Duck

This duck is rubbed with spices, dried, plumped up with air and baked, so that the meat is of melt-in-the-mouth consistency and the skin is crisp. Burgundy and Pinot Noir, with some age, works and so does a good bottle of Châteauneuf du Pape or Rioja, but for something different, do try a sparkling Shiraz.

CHINA
BEIJING

Beijing, or Mandarin, cuisine has an all-embracing food history: the Mongols introduced mutton; pork became popular in the Qing Dynasty; Shandong contributed quick-frying techniques and the use of onions; and from the Huaiyang, Jiangsu and Zhejiang cuisines came many more culinary influences. Chefs from the far reaches of China came to the capital to concoct novel dishes to appease jaded royal palates and, over several dynasties, Beijing banquet-style cuisine evolved.

Cold Appetizer

The cold appetizer platter comprises at least four items from a selection including pickled spicy cucumbers, seaweed salad, spicy beef tendons, pickled fish, drunken chicken, jellyfish salad, and different types of mock duck or chicken. The accompanying wine has to be versatile and impartial. Try Cava, Prosecco, and New World sparkling wines—all with palate cleansing properties; or try a lightly sweet spätlese Riesling.

Sautéed Fish Slices

Tastewise, this dish is quite complex, with flavors of chili, garlic, ginger, vinegar, soy, sesame, and rice wine. It is therefore advisable to opt for a wine that lets the dish take the lead in terms of flavor. Chenin Blanc, dry or lightly sweet, is ideal, and so is a Verdelho, round and sometimes lightly sweet with balanced acidity

Beijing Sweet and Sour Pork

In contrast to the classic Cantonese sweet and sour dish, the Beijing version is less fruity—it omits pineapple—but instead green peppers and onions are used. Often, it's cooked with juicy tender pork loin. The wine does not have to be so characterful as in the case of the Cantonese dish. Try a Prosecco, a Cava, or an off-dry spätlese Riesling.

Fire Pot Lamb

Lamb cooked in a pot with sesame paste, chopped pickled chives, fermented beancurd, soy sauce, chili sauce, shrimp oil, sesame oil, and Shaoxing wine is far from subtle. Pick something with similar oomph such as a New World Chardonnay from a warm region—southern California or a big oaky alcoholic Australian Chardonnay. Côtes Rôtie is the red wine of choice here.

Mongolian Lamb

Although the Mongolian sauce can be strong, the flavors of the grilled lamb, its textures and its taste are upfront enough such that they can be matched by wines with sufficient tannin. Argentinean Malbec, Chilean Carménère or young Bordeaux find their place here.

Peking Chicken

Chicken is dusted with flour and then deepfried till golden brown and crisp but then warmed up with a sauce made of ginger, soy, and wine. Enjoy with any crisp white wine with a little texture. Pinot Blanc, Alsace Pinot Gris, and Marsanne are good bets.

Diced Ham with Crystal Sugar

Ham steamed with rock sugar and Chinese dates goes best with Pinot Gris that is off-dry or lightly sweet. It can also be paired with a sweeter Gewürztraminer Vendange Tardive (late harvest) but it will lend the ham a lychee-rose flavor.

Tripe

Tripe is a popular snack in Beijing. There is pot-stewed tripe (luzhu), or quick-fried mutton tripe (bao du), that is enjoyed with sesame sauce. Some tripe may even be stirfried with chicken gizzard. Whatever the style, tripe has a unique taste akin to liver but, if well prepared, picks up the taste of the sauce or gravy. If it's a tripe stew, uncork Pinot Noir, Rioja, Barolo, or Bordeaux. Otherwise, serve a Chardonnay.

CANTON

Climatically, Guangdong (Canton) is amenable to the cultivation of rice and vegetables. Fresh seafood bounty comes from the region's hundreds of miles of coastline. In the Cantonese kitchen, the emphasis is on the natural flavors of fresh ingredients. The essence of taste of Cantonese is clear, light, crisp, and fresh, and the same qualities should be looked for in the choice of accompanying wine.

Steamed Seafood with Soy and Ginger

Fish, lobster, prawns or any other crustacean, pairs well with a dry Riesling with delicate citrus and floral aromas. Its tangy acidity, can be called upon to be the counterpoint to the seafood with overtones of salty soy and sharp ginger flavors. Sauvignon Blanc could work here too if the sauce is robust (e.g. black beans), as long as the wine's grassy or asparagus overtones do not overshadow flavors of the food. A Graves from Bordeaux will have toned down Sauvignon flavors because of the addition of Semillon in the blend, and is your wine of choice.

Preserved Salted Duck

When salt is the main component of a dish (preserved salted duck, fish, chicken or pork), sweet wine offers an interesting contrast but you can also venture further afield with a tangy white. Salt-cooked chicken, typically a whole chicken buried in heated salt till well done, can be matched this way too. Monbazillac, auslese, spätlese, and late-harvest wines have a place here.

Sweet and Sour

With sweet and sour prawns, fish and pork, the match is made for the sauce. The wine has to be either quite strong or, if it is subtle such as a Champagne, there should be some sweetness to carry off the match or the wine will taste sour and flat. Chardonnay and Viognier as white wines are a good choice but a demi-sec Champagne is the best pick.

Slow-boiled Soups

Wintermelon, snow fungus, pork or game; it does not matter what the soup will be composed of. The essence of the soup is that it is clear and savory. Such soups are best enjoyed on their own but if you must, a sparkling sweet wine—Italian Spumante or lightly sweet German Sekt— could work here.

Braised Abalone

Cooked till tender and served in a clear brown sauce flavored with Chinese cabbage, dried scallops, straw mushrooms and/or Chinese black mushrooms. Grüner Veltliner with pepper nuances, or a Riesling will be befitting for this dish, although given the savory nature of its taste, a red wine such as Merlot could be ventured.

Roast Goose

Tender goose with crispy skin is usually served with soy sauce or a hoisin–chili sauce. Enjoy with Zinfandel or Primitivo if red wines are the preference. Chardonnay and White Burgundy is also good here.

Beef Stew

Although different from a Western stew, nevertheless this is a beefy-tasting dish. Turnips and carrots are replaced by Chinese radish; black bean sauce, garlic, star anise, five spice, and some Chinese wine make up the flavor. Beef brisket, chuck, round, or shank may feature in this dish. The protein and fat in the meat and stew are natural partners for wines with tannin and a bit of bite. This is the domain of Barolo, young Bordeaux, Vino Nobile di Montepulciano, Dolcetto and other chewy wines with acidity and tannin.

Iron-plate Beef

Beef fillet cooked on a hot iron plate, with a brown sauce made up of bamboo shoots and mushrooms or onions and ginger—with lots of umami— pairs well with a Cabernet Sauvignon, Bordeaux, Syrah, and Petit Verdot.

SICHUAN / HUNAN

Sichuan cuisine enjoys a reputation of being spicy and pungent. There are also sweet, sour, salty, and tongue-numbing (Sichuan pepper) tastes. Food-preservation techniques such as pickling, salting, drying, and smoking have added to the repertoire of tastes. Nearby Hunan food is similar because its residents believe that consuming hot peppers help "remove" dampness and cold in their bodies. In Hunan, like in Sichuan, game, fish, shrimp, crab, and turtle are all cooked to various flavors of hot and sour, or with fragrant aromas, and with a distinctive oiliness.

Kung Po Chicken

A classic dish featuring tastes of sweet and sour with chili spiciness, and a complexity of flavor from the garlic, scallions, peanuts, Shaoxing wine, vinegar, soy, and peppercorns. Westernized versions feature brown beans and some hoisin. Whatever the version, off-dry wines work best. The best choices are spätlese, Chenin Blanc, and Moelleux wines from the Loire Valley. Even Lambrusco, a lightly sweet red wine, is worth a gamble.

Tea-smoked Duck

A popular dish from Sichuan, duck marinated with Sichuan pepper and Shaoxing or rice wine is steamed then smoked with tea leaves and twigs, sometimes with camphor wood, and finally deep-fried. A Côtes du Rhone red wine makes a wonderful mate here.

Spicy Cucumber Salad

Crunchy cucumber pieces are tossed in hot oil flavored with fried chilies, Sichuan pepper, and nutty sesame oil, then cooled. Refreshing, as well as nutty and fiery, serve with a glass of sweet wine served very cold.

Hot and Sour Soup

Ground pepper tingles in the mouth and sour Chinkiang black vinegar adds a sharp counterpoint to the flavors of mushrooms, ham, bamboo shoots, sea cucumber, and soy. While most wines will simply fall away, it is a sweet wine that can handle the soup: Barsac, Passito, late harvest or even lightly sweet wines.

Cold Chicken in Fragrant Rice Wine

Steamed chicken with glutinous-rice wine and flavored with sesame oil is a delicious dish and its flavor can only be mirrored by the nutty and characterful taste of a Sherry. Choose between sweet (pale, medium) and dry (Oloroso, Fino) Sherries.

Barbecued Lamb Chops

The lamb is marinated in hoisin sauce, soy sauce, Sherry, chili oil, rice vinegar, onions, and finely chopped garlic, and then grilled. The wine choices are aplenty here and they are all red, some have a red fruited edge, others, the smokiness or leather-earth nuances of bottle age: Hermitage, Shiraz, Grenache, Tempranillo, Zinfandel, St Emilion, Malbec, and even Tannat.

Hunan Crispy Duck

Hunan duck is seasoned with peppercorns, star anise, fennel, and other spices, then steamed and finally deep-fried. The two wine choices here are both from Burgundy: a rich, peachy Meursault if you like white or a fruity but silky Volnay red.

Hunan Spicy Frog's Legs

The frog legs are stir-fried with green peppers, then the whole preparation is glazed with a light reddish-brown sauce. The hot sauce has a slight kick, but is not overwhelming. Red Recioto della Valpolicella is an intriguing partner otherwise a Torcolato or any sweet wine is an attractive alternative.

Xiao Long Bao

Shanghainese xiao long bao
is a steamed, meat-filled bun
with unleavened skin that
is dipped in a vinegar sauce
accented with fresh ginger.
A dry Semillon from Australia's
Hunter Valley brings to the
match a palate-cleansing
effect.

SHANGHAI

Shanghai cuisine is epitomized by the use of alcohol. Fish, eel, crab, and chicken are rendered "drunk" by liberal lashings of spirits and often the dish is served raw. Salted meats and preserved vegetables are also commonly used to spice up the dish. "Red cooking" is a popular style of braising and stewing meats and vegetables in this region.

Spicy Jellyfish
Here you have to match the wine to the coriander, nutty sesame oil, and garlic-chili dressing. A good wine match can be found in a New World Pinot Blanc. Otherwise, try pink wines such as Spanish Rosato and Italian Cerasuolo.

Sautéed Crabs with Noodles
The crab is stirfried in ginger and garlic and then braised with stock and soy, wine, oyster sauce, chives, and served with noodles. Savory and robust, the crab and a New World Chardonnay with a buttery texture and tropical fruit-citrus flavors are soulmates here.

Spicy Chicken Wings
Pickled in wine, beancurd gravy, and water chestnut, the chicken is deepfried, then bathed in chili oil and garnished with peanuts. This finger food calls for something refreshing such as a Cremant d'Alsace or a Prosecco.

Beggar's Chicken
Wrapped in lotus leaves and clay-baked, this chicken is tender and delicate in taste. Complement the textures and contrast the taste with a Trebbiano or Pinot Gris white or a Côtes du Rhone red.

Pork & Fermented Beancurd
The red fermented beancurd, augmented with oyster sauce, wine, and garlic, takes the flavor lead here, regardless of the cut of pork. Pair for the spicy-salty-cheesy taste with an Amarone, unique for its bitter-sweet flavors and whose ripe tannins and gush of fruit easily takes up with the pork. Alternative wines include Macvin du Jura and Banyuls.

FUJIAN / ANHUI / SHANDONG

Oyster Omelet
Any sparkling wine—Cava, Sekt, Mousseux, Methode Champenoise—will bring a lively edge to the pairing. The effervescence contrasts the texture of the omelet; the acidity strikes a balance with the soy or fish sauce seasonings; the wine's lemony tartness takes to the oyster's salty steely-briny flavors like a squeeze of lemon or splash of mignonette sauce.

Buddha Jumps Over The Wall
This is a complex Fujian (Hokkien) dish made of shark's fin and lip, fish maw, abalone, squid, sea cucumber, chicken, duck, pork tripe and leg, minced ham, mutton elbow, dried scallop, winter bamboo shoots, and mushrooms, all cooked separately then assembled, alcohol added, and simmered. Let the dish take the lead and serve a generic blended white wine such as Sauvignon Blanc–Chardonnay or a Chenin Blanc–Sauvignon Blanc–Colombard.

Li Hongzhang Hotchpotch
Named after a Chinese official who hosted a banquet for his American allies, this Anhui stew is composed of sea cucumber, squid, tofu, ham, mushroom, and chicken. A peppery, Petite Sirah makes the match.

Stewed Chicken
This rich Shandong dish is befitting of a grand aged wine: a Burgundy, fine old Bordeaux or Barolo.

Shandong Braised Sea Cucumbers with Scallions
With jelly-like consistency in brown sauce with savory onion gravy, this dish is matched texturally and for taste with a lightly sweet Gewürztraminer.

Tandoori Chicken

Mellow and smoky chicken cooked in a
tandoor calls for light-bodied red wines
(Gamay or Pinot Noir) or perhaps a fuller-
bodied Zinfandel. White wines with hints of
oak (Chardonnay or Fumé Blanc) also work as
they downplay the dish's smokiness.

INDIA
NORTH INDIA

Sweetly aromatic dishes such as those found on Moghul dining tables love light-bodied, fruit-forward whites, reds or rosés, which balance the food's fruitiness and parry its sweetness. Dishes heavy on spice (not chili) can be paired with sharp, young, light-bodied generic whites as the acid helps pare down the spice. Dao or Portuguese white wines with a lemon zest are perfect here.

Dhansak

A Parsi dish, made with lamb or other meat and featuring vegetables and various dhal. In taste, it is hot, sweet, and sour. So for tangy Dhansak, choose Beaujolais, Montepulciano d'Abruzzo and any pink wine. The wine's fruit will match the tang in the dish whilst the wine tannins sit happily alongside the dish's fatty texture.

Korma

Of all the curries, the korma is the most delicate, using yogurt and cream as base for meats such as lamb or chicken. Match its flavors with a cherry flavored New World Pinot Noir or a Sicilian Nero d'Avola.

Rogan Josh

Spiced lamb is a classic Kashmiri dish. Serve a Shiraz or Syrah that will enhance the taste of the lamb and that will not be overcome by the strong flavors.

Mughlai

This Persian-Turkish cooking style incorporates in the dish, lashings of ginger, ground almonds, yogurt, and cream and the dish is mild in taste but rich in texture. You can serve Shiraz, Pinot Noir, Tempranillo and a selection of white wines aged in oak, such as Chardonnay, Fumé Blanc, Viognier, and Pinot Blanc.

Pasanda

The thinly sliced lamb fillets with ground almonds, cardamom pods, puréed tomatoes, and cream, is the perfect foil for big red wines. Choose from Barolos, Bordeaux, and Gran Reserva Riojas.

Murg Makhani

For this Punjabi butter chicken, the wine choices range from a buttery Chardonnay to a fruity rosé, to even a light red wine such as Pinot Noir.

Jalfrezi

Once a stir-fry of leftover cold roasted meat and potatoes, jalfrezi has evolved into a stir-fry of meat with green peppers, onions, and plenty of green chilies. Serve an ice-cold rosé wine or something sweet and syrupy such as a Riversaltes from south of France or Austrian beerenauslese Riesling.

Saag Meat / Seafood

This classic curry featuring tender green leaves such as spinach, mustard greens, and fresh fenugreek leaves and either chicken, prawn, or lamb will be well spiced with a thick gravy. The ground vegetables play more than a textural role. They can react adversely with tannic wines so serve lightly sweet wines such as Gewürztraminer and Moscato.

Keema

Keema is a delightful mince of lamb with curry spices and green peas or potatoes or other vegetables, stirfried and served with Indian breads. Alternatively, it can be formed into a kebab. Barbecued or not, this dish calls for a juicy red wine such as a Grenache.

Kashmiri Yakhni

Kashmiri lamb stew is brimming with flavors of aniseed, cumin, cardamom, ginger, and curd. The wine has to accommodate this complex mélange of tastes and yet not be overcome. A red Côtes du Rhone Villages is the best choice here.

Masala Shalgam

Zinfandel is the best bet for this Punjabi spiced turnip dish served with rice or roti.

Hyderabadi Biryani

This very popular biryani dish
is essentially mutton marinated
in curd and then cooked along
with basmati rice, curd, onions,
spices, lemon, and saffron
in a sealed pot over coals.
Fragrant and steaming hot, it is
served with a chutney of curd
and onions and a green chili
curry or tomato based curry.
It needs a wine that is neutral
but friendly such as Verdelho or
Pinot Gris.

SOUTH AND EAST INDIA / SRI LANKA

Food from the south, with its emphases on coconut and lively tasting tamarind, appears deceptively easy when it comes to wine pairing. Choose different wines to match for flavors and sensations. Certain California Chardonnays take on shaved-coconut flavors from the wood ageing mirror the coconut flavors in southern curries. The tanginess of tamarind and other souring agents can be matched with fruity wines.

Kerala Chicken Stew

A young and powerful Cabernet Sauvignon would be the ideal choice to accompany a peppery Keralan chicken stew, just as a similar wine might be served in the West with a black pepper steak.

Naadan Chicken Curry

This dry curry from Kerala with aromas of curry leaves and, sometimes, mustard seeds and lime leaves needs a crisp white wine as contrast: Pinot Blanc, Pinot Grigio or a Trebbiano.

Goan-style Mussels

Fried mussels with ginger, garlic, chilies, turmeric, cumin, and the nutty taste of coconut call for a wine that echoes some of its flavors—opt for an oak-aged Chardonnay.

Goan Prawn Curry

A little sour from the tamarind, a little creamy from the coconut, and with the aromatic melange of cumin, coriander, and turmeric, this curry needs a wine that will not clash head-on with its flavors. Venture a tangy sweet Riesling Spätlese, that will also handle the hot chili spice.

Sorportel

This spicy dish of pork, with some liver, that is enjoyed with sannas—a steamed rice cake made from ground rice, coconut, sugar, and salt—is best washed down with a Beaujolais or Gamay-based wine, served cold.

Chicken Cafreal

This Goan-style chicken marinated in chilies, lime juice (or vinegar), and spices, is either deepfried, barbecued or roasted. The refreshing taste of Rosé d'Anjou is mandatory.

Kutchhi Bhindi

Hot and sour okra—or ladies fingers'—cooked Gujerati-style, is flavored with cumin, garlic, and chili and gets its tartness from lemon juice. A medium-bodied white wine, not too tart fits the bill here. Choose from Sauvignon Blancs and even Gewürztraminers from the New World.

Bengali Fish Curry

Fish cooked with a paste of mustard seeds, chili, and some coriander, is a simple three-ingredient dish yet the dish is complete in its taste. Accompany with a dry Cava or sparkling wine.

Aloo Poshto

This Bengali dish is made by frying potato cubes and poppy seeds in chili and turmeric with a garnish of cilantro. A Pinot Noir takes well to the taste of cilantro and the sprightliness of the chili, as long as the dish is not searingly chili hot.

Jaffna Seafood Soup

Like bouillabaisse, this Tamil dish is made from a variety of fish and crustaceans. However this stew's secondary flavors come from the use of jackfruit, tapioca, and tamarind making it sour salty so a Riesling would not be out of place here.

Sri Lankan Beef Smore

This famous Dutch Burgher dish from Sri Lanka is essentially a beef stew flavored with onion, garlic, ginger, tomato, cloves, cardamom, cinnamon, curry powder, fenugreek, lemongrass, fennel powder, coriander, and chili and cooked in coconut milk. This hearty dish is mellow in taste. Shiraz or a Soave Superiore are good bets to serve with it.

Montepulciano is a grape of the Abruzzo region in Italy. Montepulciano d'Abruzzo should not be confused with Vino Nobile de Montepulciano or Rosso di Montepulciano. These wines, made from Sangiovese, are named after the charming hilltop town of Montepulciano in Tuscany.

Cumi Bakar

Of West Javanese origin, barbecued or fried squid is slathered with sweet thick rich kecap manis. Cut through the sweetness and the texture with an aromatic wine such as Sauvignon Blanc or a Spanish Albariño.

INDONESIA

If the islands of Maluku, the Spice Islands, introduced to the world the native Indonesian spices, other cultures too have contributed to Indonesian cuisine throughout its history. The Spanish brought chilies, the Arabs and Indian traders introduced more spices, and the Chinese contributed cooking methods, noodles, soy sauce, and other herbs. Dishes tend to spicy and a little sweet, which is something to consider when choosing a wine.

Ayam Masak Madu

This honey chicken dish is lightly sweet and sour. Such dishes call for a young Chardonnay that has pineapple, lychee, peach or smoky-butter aromas.

Ayam Taliwang

Originating from Nusa Tenggara (east of Bali), this is a popular spicy dish of grilled chicken. Have it with a light red such as the Cabernet Franc-based Chinon from the Loire Valley.

Sup Buntut

Oxtail in a clear soup is savory and a little spicy and beefy. It calls for a generic white or red wine. Another version is roasted oxtail served with a barbecue sauce, which would work with a Zinfandel or Shiraz.

Nasi Goreng

There is no one recipe for Indonesian fried rice but the standard dish will have been stirfried with eggs, meatballs, assorted vegetables, and chicken, beef or shrimp. The rice is made brown and lightly sweet with kecap manis, so a lightly sweet wine such as spätlese Riesling works here.

Nasi Goreng Istimewa

Istimewa, or special, fried rice features prawns, chicken satay, acar, prawn crackers and a fried egg and it is best accompanied by a light but fruity red wine such as a Montepulciano d'Abruzzo.

Pempek Palembang

This Sumatran deepfried fishball dish is sweet from palm sugar, sour from vinegar and tamarind, and served as soup. Mirror the tastes with a demi-sec Champagne.

Ayam Tuturaga

Originally featuring turtle meat, this Manado curry now uses chicken. It is fragrant from the use of pandanus, lemongrass, kaffir, cumin, ginger, and garlic, and is thickened with eggs and candlenuts. Pinot Blanc accompanies it well.

Babi Guling

Babi guling is a juicy, crunchy and absolutely delectable Balinese-style roast pig that is served with gravy over rice with some chili and vegetables. Pinot Noir, Ribera del Duero or even a white such as a Viognier will enable you to savor the roast pig.

Sayur Asem

This tamarind-flavored dish often features melinjo leaves, sweet corn, and young papaya, together with peanuts, in a clear soup. The tamarind imparts a sour flavor and a Pinot Gris is the wine to go for.

Udang Belado

Fried prawns with chili sauce requires either the cleansing action of a crisp Riesling or Argentinean Torrontés, or a richly sweet wine that will handle the chili such as a Muscat. Otherwise a lightly sweet sparkling wine works too—try a German Sekt or demi-sec Vouvray.

Lumpia Semarang

These Javanese spring rolls are prepared with cooked bamboo shoots and chicken or prawn, and sometimes boiled quail eggs. The dipping sauce is made from coconut sugar, vinegar and garlic and benefits from a robust sweet wine: Port, Rasteau or Madeira.

Tahu Telor

Serve an Australian late-harvest Riesling or botrytised wine with this sweet and spicy dish of beancurd cubes and egg.

Soto Ayam

This chicken soup, with beansprouts and potato croquettes goes with a lightly sweet and sparkling German Sekt. The wine's bubbles are a contrast to the soup's texture whilst the light sweetness highlights the soup's savoriness.

Sushi

Uncork any tangy, crisp white wine when dining on seafood-topped nigiri-zushi, maki-zushi, and temaki as the wine has to complement the fish like a squeeze of lemon, but it also has to overcome the vinegar in the rice base. Best choices include dry Riesling, Grüner Veltliner, Chenin Blanc, Colombard, and Assyrtiko. Watch out for the wasabi!

JAPAN

Japanese wine drinkers have been at the forefront of the wine revolution in Asia. Although the tradition of drinking sake with Japanese food has not diminished in popularity, it is now commonplace for New World and European wines to be enjoyed with Japanese meals. From the freshness of fish and the crispness of tempura to the hearty nabemono (one-pot cooked dishes) and smoke-nuanced grilled yakimono dishes, the emphasis is frequently on just a few flavors, and identifying and responding to those flavors is the key to successful food and wine pairings.

Sashimi (lean fish)

Try to match the taste and texture of the raw fish. Lean fish including lobster, octopus, oyster, prawn, sea bass, sea bream, squid, swordfish, trout, and tuna have stronger tastes so you could serve an aged white wine such as a brut Champagne or Chablis. Otherwise go for Pinot Gris/Grigio, Viognier, or Soave Classico that are rich in texture and taste.

Sashimi (fatty fish)

Fatty fish like salmon and tuna belly can handle light red wines, unoaked red wine, generic red Burgundy, Pinot Noir, Barbera, Beaujolais, and Chinon.

Sashimi (oily fish)

Oily fish flavors range from subtle to strong—think herring, horse mackerel, pike, sardine, and yellowtail. Serve juicy fruity wines with stronger fish but try also a good Pinotage from South Africa that has slight saline tastes.

Shojin Ryori

This special Zen Buddhist cuisine features tofu, vegetables, and non-meat dishes. Because of the nature of the food, flavors and tastes are quite delicate so the chosen wine needs to be easygoing and not overwhelming. Go for neutral wines such as unoaked Chardonnay, Chasselas, Colombard, Pinot Grigio, or Trebbiano.

Seaweed salad

Japanese seaweed salads may be dressed with a sesame-soy-vinegar (nutty) sauce or feature ginger or onion. If the dressing is strong, a lightly sweet wine will do well. Moscato or Gewürztraminer are good bets.

Beef Teppanyaki

This is the realm of steak so you can have robust or tannic wines here—think big Bordeaux, Cahors, Barolo, Gran Reserva Rioja, New World Reserve Cabernet Sauvignon and even Malbec, Tannat and Dolcetto. Prefer a white? Then choose Chardonnay or Pinot Blanc, with lots of oak ageing.

Beef or Pork Sukiyaki

The stew, made with lightly caramelized sugar, mirin-dashi (wine and kelp or shiitake stock) is best matched by wines with a definite sweetness such as Barsac or late harvests.

Shabu-shabu

Meat cooked in a simmering broth then dipped in either a lemony ponzu or sesame-nutty sauce takes to the wonderful hints of orange and apricots in a Hungarian Tokaji or the pear and citrus sweet notes in a Canadian ice wine. Alternatively, try a sweet Sherry—the nuttiness of the shabu-shabu's sesame sauce responds to the wine's strong, full-bodied character, creating a match of textures.

Yakitori

Yakitori refers to chicken but we can include gizzards, mushrooms, meat balls, quail eggs, liver and more for it is the grilled meat taste and the yakitori sauce that we are matching. So, not surprisingly, the dish's smoky aromas, reminiscent of campfires, and rustic, savory flavors, form an easy affinity with the peppery notes of the Shiraz grape. The Rhone Valley's Cornas, the inky, tarry and jammy Syrah, transcends the flavors of the hot grill to make a robust liaison with most varieties of yakitori.

Gyudon

Literally "rice in a bowl," that is topped with beef and onion that has been simmering in a mildly sweet sauce flavored with soy and mirin. A New

Yakizakana

This simple grilled fish dish, often prepared at home, usually has a pronounced fishy taste and also the crunch of crispy skin, allied with the round fat texture of fish such as mackerel. Crisp, tangy wines such as Sauvignon Blanc–Semillon blends, Burgundian Aligote or Argentinean Torrontés work well here; while they take second place in flavor to the grilled tastes, their tanginess lessens the fishiness of the mackerel. Alternatively, try a fino Sherry, the traditional match in Spain.

World blended red wine, not too tannic, pairs well with the savory sweet flavors of the dish. Choose from Cabernet-Shiraz, Cabernet-Malbec and other variations.

Tonkatsu

Tonkatsu ("ton" means pig and "katsu" means cutlet) was invented in the Ginza, Tokyo. The deepfried pork cutlet, crunchy on the outside, moist and meaty on inside gets its main flavoring ingredient from the sauce (soy, sake, mustard, Worcestershire, and ketchup). The sauce can be light or piquant, sour-sweet and heavy so choose an appropriate wine: a light dry generic white wine with palate cleansing qualities or a sweet white wine that can stand up to the sauce. Otherwise, red wines such as Saint-Nicolas-de-Bourgueil (Cabernet Franc) or Beaujolais can be served.

Tempura

Iced Port works very nicely with this deepfried treat, the sweetness of the Port enveloping the tongue and taking the edge off the heat of the tempura that is always eaten just out of the frying pan. If Port is too alcoholic and sweet for your tastes, take another route—select a tangy, crisp dry wine such as Chenin Blanc. Alternatively, Austrian Grüner Veltliner with white peppery aromas and dry Riesling-like character renders it a fitting partner to tempura.

Teriyaki

Only a sweet wine with honey-orange flavors such as a Muscat de Beaumes de Venise will pair with this dish of sweet soy glazed meat or seafood. Opt for the lighter Coteaux du Layon from the Loire valley if the seafood is delicate.

Zaru Soba

This summertime favorite in Japan features cold buckwheat noodles, presented on a bed of wrapped ice, and served with a dip of soy sauce topped with scallions, nori, and wasabi. Most medium-full bodied whites, in particular Chardonnay, Pinot Blanc, and New World Sauvignon Blanc, work with this refreshing dish, while responding to the scallions and wasabi in the dip.

Soba / Udon / Somen

Noodles such as soba, udon, and somen, and the Chinese-influenced ramen, served hot with a savory soy sauce can forge an association with the oak in red wine. The same rule applies to yakisoba and yaki-udon (fried noodles).

Gyoza

Similar to Chinese pot-stickers, gyoza are dumplings filled with pork, cabbage, scallion, garlic or garlic chives, and ginger. Gyoza may be served boiled or deepfried, but the usual way is to steam-fry them so that they are crispy on the bottom and smooth and slippery on the top. The accompanying wine should be a Spanish Albariño or Italian Vermentino.

Unagi

Grilling is the most common way to cook unagi (eel). Kabayaki is the glaze of sugar, soy, and mirin used for grilling. To match the sweet, caramelized smoky eel flavors, uncork an oaked, aged Chardonnay.

Nasu No Inakani

Eggplant or aubergine stewed in soy, sugar, sesame oil, and a little chili is best enjoyed warm with some rice. A light white wine such as Pinot Grigio is a good counterpoint to the salty taste of this vegetable dish. A similar wine would work with other vegetable dishes of kabu no ichiyazuke (salt pickled turnip) and ninjin no amani (sweet cooked carrots).

Nikujaga

This stew of thinly sliced beef, minced meat or pork with potatoes, onions and other vegetables is home-cooked comfort food. Serve an equally affable wine such as a rosé.

Kani-su

This crab and cucumber salad, is dressed with ginger juice, vinegar, soy, sugar, and dashi. Attain an alliance of the sweet and tart with spätlese Riesling.

Soboro-don

This comfort food of minced chicken seasoned with mirin and soy gets a little heat from added ginger juice. The chopstick-scrambled eggs help to complete the taste. Pink or rosé wines with strawberry and fruit punch flavors from Provence are ideal.

Daifuku

Mochi or glutinous rice cakes filled with sweetened red bean paste (an) or white bean paste (shiro an) is seldom overly sweet. Lovely with an Alsace 'vendange tardive' Pinot Gris.

Yukhoe

Korean steak tartare but with soy sauce, sugar, salt, sesame oil, scallion, ground garlic, sesame seeds, black pepper, and the juice of nashi pear. Beaujolais will take second place in the flavor match but nevertheless does work.

KOREA

Three jang (seasonings) represent Korean flavors: doen-jang (soybean paste), gochu-jang (red chili paste), and gan-jang (soy sauce). Other ingredients, such as sesame oil, garlic, fresh chili, chili flakes, and chili powder, hint at the heavy seasoning of many Korean dishes. Certainly no Korean meal would be complete without kimchi, a fermented condiment. Kimchi's hot and spicy taste is used to stimulate the appetite, ward off illness, and add texture to a meal. Koreans enjoy kimchi made from white cabbage (baek), cucumber (oisobaegi), radish (chonggak-mu) and more.

Saengseon Hoe
A dry white wine, from Sauvignon Blanc and Riesling to Tocai would work with this dish of thinly sliced raw fish as long as the fish is dipped sparingly in the accompanying spicy pungent cho-go-chu-jang sauce.

Gom-tang
This stewed meat and tripe soup contains beef brisket, beef entrails, bones, and tripe, boiled together and then served with rice, scallions, and chili. A fruity red wine such as Shiraz or Zinfandel can be served here.

Japchae
Vermicelli noodles with beef and vegetables such as dried black mushrooms, onions, carrots, scallions, bell pepper, garlic, sesame oil, and soy is nutty, savory, and sweet at the same time. A chilled sweet wine such as an Orange Muscat will round out the pungency of the dish. Otherwise try any Muscats (brown, red, or the fortified Beaumes de Venise).

Bimbimbap
Rice with beef, vegetables, and salad with a garlic sweet soy and sesame tastes, is augmented with pepper and some chili paste. The whole mixture is quite delicious and the characterful tastes can be matched by a fruity, full bodied red wine or a Viognier.

Kimchi Jjigae
Stewed pork/beef/anchovies and kimchi makes for an aromatic combination that is heady with garlic, soy, and pepper tastes. Go for a Chilean blended red wine here.

Beef Bulgogi
Beef marinated in soy, garlic, brown sugar, wine, and nashi pear, then barbecued is best enjoyed when it is wrapped in a lettuce leaf with some raw chili and garlic. The taste is at once sharp, savory, smoky, and beefy. Southern Italian Primitivo with light tannins yet with concentrated berry flavors makes a good match. Try also a Malbec from Argentina.

Doenjang Jjigae
This soybean-paste stew might contain tofu, clam meat, pork, beef, or simply zucchini. Not only the malty taste of the fermented bean paste, garlic, and pepper powder but the anchovies used has to be considered. If it's beef, red meat, or chicken, a fruity Merlot will play second fiddle in tastes. If it's seafood or tofu, venture a Chenin Blanc, Pineau de la Loire, or a Steen from South Africa.

Samgyeopsal
Thick, fatty slices of pork belly meat flavored with garlic, salt, and sesame oil and grilled, are eaten with lettuce, chili paste (gochujang) and/or soybean paste (doenjang) and sometimes with chilies and slices of garlic, all at the same time. This is the domaine of big wines such as Shiraz and Zinfandel.

Fish
Thinly sliced raw fish (domi) with a spicy gochu-jang goes with Vouvray Moelleux. If pan-fried with salt or in batter (chonyu) the fish finds its match with a creamy, vanilla-tasting Pinot Blanc.

Samge-Tang
The taste of sweet dates, ginger, garlic, herbal ginseng, and savory chicken in a soup can be contrasted by a lightly sweet wine with a hint of effervescence such as a Moscato d'Asti.

If kimchi is the overriding taste, consider serving Port or a Manzanilla Sherry.

Roti Canai

Roti canai (in Malaysia) or roti prata (in Singapore) is a thin dough pan-fried on a griddle till it is golden brown. Murtabak is the same, filled with minced mutton, garlic, egg, and onion, and fried on a griddle until it turns golden brown. Both are served with curry and the most suitable wine is a sweet sparkling wine such as Asti.

MALAYSIA & SINGAPORE

Malaysian and Singaporean cuisine reflects the melting pot of ethnic groups that populate both countries: predominantly Malay, Chinese, and Indian, with influences from the colonial Portuguese, Dutch, and British, early mercantile Arabs, and neighboring Thais and Indonesians. Some dishes remain true to their cultural origins while others are a delicious blend of ingredients from several ethnic backgrounds. Wine is popular in both countries, and specialist wine merchants and wine bars are mushrooming.

Ayam Goreng

Chicken marinated with turmeric and curry powder and then deepfried is at once crunchy and savory. Serve with Cava or a New World sparkling wine. This wine also works with ayam percik roasted chicken.

Nasi Lemak

This popular dish of coconut rice with chicken or beef rendang, fried anchovies, peanuts, boiled or fried egg, chili sambal, and cucumber is spicy and sweet so try an ice-cold Austrian beerenauslese.

Nasi Goreng Kampung

This traditional, village-style fried rice is usually very spicy. Think Malvasia, Marsala or any sweet wine here.

Ikan Asam Pedas

This sour and hot fish dish is simply the perfect foil for a Sauvignon Blanc or Fumé Blanc.

Ikan Panggang / Ikan Bakar

Fish marinated with a spice paste, wrapped in banana leaves and then charcoal grilled is a Malay classic. Its flavors are smoky and quite strong. Pick a wine that will not be overwhelmed such as a Chardonnay aged in oak.

Sambal Petai

This dish contains bitter (some would say foul-smelling) beans in a sweetish chili sauce, and sometimes crispy fried anchovies are added. Consumed with rice and other dishes, the wine should play a secondary role. Wash everything down with a chilled "blush" wine or White Zinfandel.

Ayam Masak Merah

Literally red-cooked chicken, this dish is spicy hot, red in color due to the chilies, and quite powerful. It calls for the quenching, watermelon flavors of a White Zinfandel.

Sotong Kunyit

Turmeric squid with sambal paste and kaffir lime leaves are cooked in light coconut cream sauce—the dish would go with a Pinot Blanc.

Lontong

Compressed rice cakes in a spicy vegetable soup is all coconuty in taste with the crunch of vegetables. Rosé is the wine of choice here.

Tahu Goreng

Fried tofu with sweet sauce is sometimes served with crushed peanuts or prawn paste. Neither versions will overpower an oak-aged Soave Classico or Spanish Albariño Barrica.

Yong Tau Foo

The taste of this Chinese bean-curd dish is dictated by the dipping sauce. Usually it is sweet and a little spicy. Because of the sweet sauce, choose a generic red wine with some residual sweetness. Try Southern European wines and New World wines from warm countries.

Satay Celup

This steamboat satay, which is unique to the historical city of Malacca, consists of raw meat, seafood or vegetables on skewers that are cooked into a boiling spicy peanut sauce. Flavors are strong here so venture a robust wine such as Port.

Bak Kut Teh

This Chinese herbal pork rib soup is usually eaten with rice, and often served with yu tiao (strips of fried dough) for dipping. Soy sauce may contain chilies and minced garlic. A fruity Merlot or Nero d'Avola will handle the spice but will also marry well with the pork dipped in the savory soy sauce.

Loh Bak

This famous Penang dish refers to meat rolls wrapped in

Hainanese Chicken Rice

The steamed chicken is enjoyed with chili, thick dark soy, and ginger hence the wine has to have character. Choose Chardonnay if dipping lightly into the sauces; pick Vouvray demi-sec if dipping boldly into the sauces; and, if the rice is topped with generous lashings of chili, ginger, and sweet soy, Sauternes makes a heavenly match.

beancurd skin and deepfried but also other morsels such as prawn fritters (heh chee), fried beancurd, octopus and century eggs with preserved ginger. The essence of taste in loh bak is its two dipping sauces—one a chili sauce and the other a starchy sauce flavored with five-spice powder. A lightly sweet wine such as spätlese Riesling or any wine with the term Moelleux on the label is the choice here.

Curry Puffs

Spice-lovers will dig the curry flavors in these spicy vegetarian/chicken/pork pies. Serve a chilled sweet Sherry.

Char Siew Rice (or noodles)

Rice or noodles, the dish with barbecued pork in a thick sauce goes best with a fruity red wine from the New World with lots of residual sugar such as Shiraz-Cabernet blends, Cabernet-Merlot blends, and Zinfandel.

Claypot Chicken

Rice rice cooked with soy sauce in a claypot, then topped with braised chicken and Chinese sausage. The oil and shiitake's umami take to Merlot or Pinotage.

Duck Rice

The braised duck with rice cooked with yam and shrimps features side dishes of braised hard-boiled eggs, preserved salted vegetables, and hard beancurd (tau kua). Taste wise, the duck predominates and so Pinot Noir has a place here.

Spicy Kelantan Chicken

The chicken is half cooked in a curry mixture of lemongrass, coconut, tamarind, ginger, chilies, and candlenuts, and then grilled over a low charcoal fire. The dish is nutty, smoky and spicy all at once. Choose an earthy or leather-nuanced wine such as Malbec, aged Zinfandel or a Barolo.

Tempeh Rendang

In this version of tempeh—in a cooked-down dry curry stew of rendang—the creamy coconut taste can take on reds such as Beaujolais or a Bardolino.

Indian Rojak

This Muslim-Indian dish of various vegetables and seafood deepfried in batter is dipped in a sweet sauce. For palate cleansing properties, a Trebbiano white wine or a blended white from Friuli, Italy works here. Alternatively, try a Chenin Blanc late harvest.

Yu Sheng (Yee Sang)

This raw fish salad with sweet, nutty and tangy sauces that is served during Chinese New Year, is best paired with a lightly sweet wine. For the celebratory spirit, uncork a demi-sec or a doux (richly sweet) Champagne.

Mango Kerabu

This spicy sweet mango salad, different from the Thai version, is made from ripe sweet mangoes. The sweet taste is tempered with a tinge of chili and lifted by fragrant cilantro. Any dry wine will taste sour alongside so venture a dessert wine: ice wine, Barsac, Moscato or late harvest Riesling.

Keripik Tempe

This crispy fried fermented soya bean cake, with flavors of coriander, garlic, and candlenuts, calls for a crisp dry white such as a Semillon.

Udang Nanas Lemak

Prawns in coconut milk with pineapple has its origins in Malacca. This creamy coconut gravy with a hint of belacan, turmeric, and galangal is quite complex tasting, if mild in terms of chili piquancy. Pair with an unoaked Chardonnay from a warm New World country, which often has tropical fruit nuances.

Chicken Wings

Serve a Merlot, preferably from California with some residual sweetness, to match hot and spicy chicken wings or any spicy sauce served with the wings. Craving a white wine? Try Gewürztraminer.

Kueh Pisang

Banana cakes with vanilla and coconut flavors are easily matched to an ice wine or Bonnezeaux.

Sambal Asam Udang

The use of tamarind, chili, sugar, and candlenuts lends this prawn dish a sweet-sour-piquant taste. Mirror the sweet and sour flavors with a Sauvignon Blanc that brings with it a grassy edge.

Ice Jelly

Jelly topped with shaved ice, lime and a choice of fruit is heavenly with a Muscat de Beaumes de Venise.

Ayam Buah Keluak

Chicken cooked with keluak nuts is a hallmark of Nyonya cooking. The bitter, strong, chocolate flavors of the nut are reminiscent of Mexican mole poblano dishes but with the heady belacan shrimp paste of the Asian palate. Rustic wines have their place here. Try the Tannat-based Madiran wine from Southwest France or any generic red.

NYONYA & EURASIAN

Nyonya (also Nonya) cuisine is the food of the Peranakan subethnic group hailing from Malacca, Singapore, and Penang. Reflecting their ethnic origins, the cuisine combines Chinese and Malay (and to a lesser extent Dutch, Portuguese, Thai, Indonesian, and Indian) ingredients and culinary styles. Eurasian cooking belongs to the Eurasian communities of Malacca and Singapore and reflects their Portuguese and Dutch origins. Both Nyonya and Eurasian dishes are often very spicy but can be enjoyed with the right wines.

Pongteh
A chicken (or pork), potato, and mushroom stew with sugarcane, fermented soybean, and Peranakan spices is quite savory and can be paired well with a Malbec.

Ang Koo Kuih
Rice-tapioca cakes of green peas are best savoured with a glass of Cream Sherry.

Se Bak
Pork loin, marinated overnight with herbs and spices, and cooked to perfection over a slow fire will take to most red wines. Shiraz–Cabernet blends, Nebbiolo, and Merlot have their place here.

Itek Tim
Also known as kiam chye ark th'ng (salted vegetable duck soup) is a duck dish with preserved mustard leaf and cabbage. It is salty with flavors of nutmeg, savory

Chinese mushrooms, tangy tomatoes, and peppercorns. This is a complex dish and the accompanying wine should be reddish and sweet. Try Marzemino, Lambrusco and Brachetto d'Acqui, failing which, White Zinfandel.

Ter Thor T'ng
Soup with pig stomach and strong white peppercorn spicing calls for a sweet wine. Any late-harvest wine, served ice cold, will play a contrasting role in taste and temperature.

Bak Wan Kepiting
This clear light soup contains hand-rolled meatballs made of crab, pork, and bamboo shoots. The flavor of the soup is pure and calls for an equally pristine wine, such as spätlese Riesling.

Stirfried Pork with Cincaluk
Cincaluk is a potent condiment made by fermenting tiny shrimps with salt, water,

and sugar. As lime juice usually is added to cincaluk dishes to brighten the taste, wines such as Vin de Savoie, Picpoul de Pinet, Shilcher or Vinho Verde can play the same role and make the marriage.

Pork Vindaloo
Originating from the Portuguese settlement of Goa in India, the meat is marinated in a blend of hot chilies, ginger, garlic, and other spices. Vinegar adds a mouth-watering tang to the dish. Try a Recioto di Soave, which is crisp and sweet and offers a good balance to the chili tang.

Pork Bostador
In local Portuguese dialect bostador means "slap". Indeed this dish leaves a fiery hotness on the cheek. Garlic, shallots, candlenuts, turmeric powder, belacan, and lots of chilies go into the making of this dish. Serve a Pineau de Charentes—

sweet yet refreshing and made from unfermented grape juice blended with Cognac.

Curry Feng
Christmas in a Eurasian home is not complete without pork mince curry (minced meat, liver, and innards). The curry is best enjoyed with a crusty baguette and a glass of Moscato. If the curry is not too spicy, a Zinfandel also works well.

Penang Fish Head Curry
Red snapper head and okra are stewed in a thick savory-sour tamarind-lemongrass-coconut gravy. The Singapore version has a thinner gravy spiced with coriander, cumin, and fenugreek. Whichever style, the wine must have some sweetness to parry the chili and also some tangy acidity to maintain balance. Blended whites such as Chenin–Verdelho, Semillon–Sauvignon Blanc or a Pessac–Léognan can work magic here.

Adobong Monok/Baboy

Chicken and/or pork adobo, braised in
pepper, garlic, soy sauce, and vinegar is
the most famous dish of the Philippines.
Serve some Minervois from France, a
Sangiovese blend from Tuscany or a
Tempranillo blend from Spain.

PHILIPPINES

Evolved over several centuries, the cuisine of the Philippines has been influenced by Indian, Malay, Chinese, Spanish, and American cooking. There is a predominating taste of either sour, salty, bitter, or sweet in the dishes and the basic flavors come from the use of sugar, fermented fish paste (bagoong), fish sauce (patis) soy sauce, vinegar (suka), coconut milk, cilantro, kalamansi lime, and tamarind.

Green Mango Salad

This salad is made up of chunks of green mango and tiny cherry tomatoes, sometimes with onions, and always with bagoong (salted shrimp fry paste). Go for a generic sparkling wine or a Riesling.

Picadillo

Spanish influences are apparent in this minced beef soup with tomatoes and pepper but the dish is localized with the use of fish sauce and cilantro. Serve a Barolo or a Bordeaux. Dry Cabernet Sauvignon from the New World also has a place here.

Kare-kare

Kare-kare is an oxtail stew with tripe that features vegetables cooked in peanut sauce (sometimes with some shrimp paste and lime juice). It has creamy, nutty, rich flavors so an Australian Shiraz, a little sweet, warm, and rich, makes the pairing, adding red berried fruit to the flavors of the stew.

Sinigang

A tamarind-flavored stew of pork, fish, or shrimp with vegetables. The taste is lightly citrussy from added lemon or patis (fish sauce) and the tamarind, and quite savory from the onion, garlic, and tomato that is added. It is a difficult dish for wine but a sweet wine such as Moscato can make the match, given the contrast the wine brings.

Torta

This local frittata can feature minced meat, onions and potatoes or lots of different vegetables and crab. If it is meat based, serve a Côtes du Rhone red while the seafood version will go well with a glass of chilled Chardonnay or Pinot Blanc.

Pork Pata Asado

A delicious dish of pork leg simmered in a pan with garlic, onions, peppercorns star anise, dark soy, sugar, and herbs such as bay leaf. Serve an Alsace Pinot Gris that can handle the sweet and savory taste as well as the fatty texture of the dish.

Barbikyu

Filipino satay is marinated, then coated with a thick sweet sauce of soy and banana ketchup (which gives it its red color) and grilled. Another version uses wine, soy, and sugar as marinade. Sublime with a thirst-quenching Spanish Rosado or Italian Rosato.

Kaldereta

This hearty stew of goat, lamb pork or beef in tomato, with olives, dill, and chili combined with cream and cheese, tastes quite Western. Choose a robust but generous wine such as a Grenache from France's South or the New World.

Pancit

In this dish, noodles are stirfried with pork, shrimp, garlic, peas, bamboo, baby corn, egg, and chives. The taste is multi dimensional given the ingredients so a wine needs to be quite characterful. Try White Port on ice.

Halo Halo

Combine caramelized sugar, milk, ice cream, red beans, yellow mung beans, banana, yam, coconut, other fruits, and pandan syrup and you get halo halo, the queen of desserts. Pair with a wine that is much sweeter, such as a Hungarian Tokaji.

Apritadang Manok

Chicken stew cooked in tomato sauce with vegetables including red bell pepper with hints of garlic and onion will accompany wines such as Chenin Blanc from South Africa and Saumur Champigny (Cabernet Franc) reds from France.

Pinks to choose from: Vin Gris, Oeil de Perdrix, Bordeaux Clairet, White Zinfandel, Loire's briskly tangy rosé, Provencal pinks, jammy Australian rosés, fruity Italian Cerasuolos, and even Champagne.

Tom Yum Goong

This classic spicy Thai soup of seafood (or chicken) can be eaten as a complete meal with noodles or rice. Redolent of lemongrass, kaffir lime, and basil, tom yum goes very well with sweet wines like Muscat and German spätlese Rieslings. The inherent sweetness in these wines coats the tongue, soothing the chili sensations and lengthening the fragrance of the herbs.

THAILAND

Ingredients such as ginger, sugar, kaffir lime leaves, cilantro, lemongrass, basil, chili, and fish sauce give Thai dishes a lively yet harmonious balance. The five fundamental flavors of the cuisine are: hot, sour, sweet, salty, and bitter/herbal. Regardless of whether you're dining on hearty fare from the northern provinces, palace cuisine or street food from Bangkok, or rich, hot curries from the southern peninsula, Thai dishes can easily be enjoyed with a variety of wines.

Miang Kham

A fun starter with drinks. Ginger, shallots, peanuts, coconut flakes, lime, dried shrimp and chilies are wrapped in betel leaves and dipped into a sweet, sour and slightly fishy sauce. The wonderful explosion of flavors requires a zesty New World Sauvignon Blanc; the lime and ginger emphasize the grassy, herbal notes of the wine. Think New Zealand.

Hor Mok

The fish meat in hor mok is mixed with chili paste and coconut milk. The spicy, creamy and custard-like richness finds its match in the bubbly Cremant d'Alsace. Alternatively, a truly magical marriage of contrasts is to be found in Sauvignon Blanc whose fruit and acidity contrasts with the creamy richness of the fish custard while its herbal, grassy notes form a liaison with kaffir lime and basil offering aromas of a Thai garden.

Kao Tang Na Tang

This fried rice-cake is usually topped with chicken cooked in a thick, creamy curry paste. The hint of vanilla from a ripe California Chardonnay aged in oak barrels will make a lovely match, playing up the fragrance of coconut in the curry sauce, and will have enough body to balance the texture and oil of the fried rice-cake.

Yum Lab Meau Nang

This spicy chicken feet salad with green chilies, garlic, cilantro, and fish sauce goes down well with a Gewürztraminer. Experience how the aromatic, spicy character of the wine adds a floral (lychee, roses) character to the salad.

Som Tum

Papaya salad and a young Soave is a marriage made in heaven. The trace of tiny bubbles that give the Soave its creamy liveliness are a textural match for the shredded, pounded and ground ingredients of the papaya salad. At the same time, the soft acids in the Soave picks up the citrus flavors of the lime and unripe papaya.

Mussaman Curry

Regardless of whether this mild yet complex curry is cooked with beef, chicken or other meat, it goes beautifully with a Merlot that lengthens the aromas of the curry while having enough presence to stand up to its texture.

Gai Ho Bai Toey

Pandan chicken is popular for its flavors of cilantro and screwpine, and smokiness from the wok-frying, Even when dipped in sour sweet fish and soy sauce, Pinot Gris—rather mild in comparison—takes the secondary role of accompanying the chicken's full-on flavors.

Ma Kue Pad Nam Prik Pao

This tasty dish of grilled egg-plants topped with a paste made from tamarind, dried shrimp, dried chilies, sugar, and onions is made for big-bodied New World Merlot—the soft tannins, sweet fruit, and round finish of the wine enhances the flavors of the dish and stands up to its texture.

Khao Yam Pak Tai

This salad is sweet, sour, piquant, aromatic, pungent, green, and refreshing. Complex flavors require straightforward wines—generic dry white wine serves as a palate cleanser. Otherwise, sweet Vendange Tardive wines with honeysuckle or tropical fruit scents will sit nicely alongside the multi-flavored dish.

Khao Niaow Ma Muang

What better wine to go with sweet sticky rice bathed in coconut milk and topped with sliced ripe mango, but a Malmsey- or Bual- Madiera, dolce Marsala or Tokaji Aszú.

Chao Tom

As you bite into the grilled shrimp on sugarcane, the sweet warm juice flavors the savory shrimp ball. A sweet wine is the order of the day as any dry wines will simply taste sour. Auslese, Barsac and ice wines rule here.

VIETNAM, LAOS, CAMBODIA & MYANMAR

The cuisines of Vietnam, Laos, Cambodia, and Myanmar (Burma) are not unlike that of Thailand, but each country has their own culinary peculiarities and they are based on unique dining traditions. While all the cuisines draw on some Thai, Khmer, and Chinese ingredients and techniques, Myanmar cuisine is also influenced by neighboring India.

Mohinga

The famous rice vermicelli in fish broth from Myanmar with onions, garlic, ginger, lemongrass, and banana-stem, served with boiled eggs, fried fish cake, and fritters is at once a mélange of savory and bright flavors. Any wine should let the food take the lead. Serve a generic blended white wine.

Ngapi Gyet

This fermented spicy fish paste or salted fish from Myanmar is added to a curry of onions, tomatoes, garlic, chili, and coriander. It is served with vegetables. The wine choice is one that should be tangy and lively. Try Frascati or Petit Chablis.

Hkauk Swè Thouk

The flavors of this Myanmar wheat noodle salad with dried shrimps, shredded cabbage, and carrots, dressed with fried peanut oil, fish sauce, and lime is not too far from the flavors of Thailand. Essentially, pick a wine with some body but which also has citrus flavors such as Pinot Gris, Pinot Blanc, or Soave.

Ga Xa

Stirfried Lemongrass chicken is a delectable zesty Vietnamese dish and dry white wines with floral and citrus overtones such as Orvieto (Italy), Vinho Verde (Portugal) or simply, a blended New World white wine can be served with confidence.

Amok Trey

Cambodian fish in a thick coconut milk with curry, wrapped in banana leaves and steamed. The texture is creamy and flavors are sweet and nutty. Pair with a Chardonnay or oak-aged Sauvignon Blanc.

Com Ga Rau Thom

In this Vietnamese rice dish with shredded chicken and herb sauce, the mint can play havoc on less than characterful wines. Serve nothing light nor any wine with delicate flavors. Go for anything fortified: Muscat de Beaumes de Venise, Vin Santo, Macvin du Jura, Pineau de Charentes, Banyuls, Port or even dry Sherry.

Pho Xao Don

Stirfried rice noodles with beef and vegetables is an alternative to the soupy Vietnamese pho. Pho xao don features a thick earthy sauce, and light reds such as Gamay, Chinon, Bourgueil, and Saint-Nicolas-de-Bourgueil find a place here.

Chim Cut Ran

Quail, marinated with ginger and wine, steamed, and then coated with honey soy sauce and fried to a crisp finds a foil in a wine such as a Prosecco or a Cremant de Die. Otherwise any sparkling wine will do: brut (dry) or demi sec (sweet), depending on preferences.

Laap

The Lao national dish (also spelled larb) is a spicy mixture of wild meat and/or fish that is served raw or cured accompanied by greens, herbs, and spices. Serve a lightly sweet wine such as Vouvray Moelleux and enjoy how the wine blends in and adds some sweetness.

Or Lam

A Laotian stew of dried buffalo meat and skin with lemongrass, chilies, and eggplant along with some fish sauce, crisp-fried pork skin, and sweet basil can take on a fruity red wine like Côtes du Rhone or Australian Shiraz.

Cha Knyey

This spicy Cambodian chicken dish is the result of stir-frying with julienned ginger root, black peppers, and fresh chili. Add some lychee flavors to the match by serving a lightly sweet Gewürztraminer, that also tames the spice.

INDEX